ONE ON A SIDE

AN EVENING WITH
SEAMUS HEANEY
& ROBERT FROST
OCTOBER 26, 2002

FOUNDATION

EDITED BY KEVIN O'CONNOR
& MARK SCHORR

BOOKMARKPRESS

LAWRENCE, MASSACHUSETTS

2008

Copyright © 2002-2008 The Robert Frost Foundation

"Out, Out –," "Mowing," "Mending Wall," "After Apple-Picking," "To Earthward," and "The Runaway" from *The Poetry of Robert Frost* edited by Edward Connery Lathem. Copyright 1916, 1923, 1930, 1934, 1939, 1969 by Henry Holt and Company, copyright 1944, 1951, 1958, 1962 by Robert Frost, copyright 1967 by Lesley Frost Ballantine from *The Poetry of Robert Frost* edited by Edward Connery Lathem. Reprinted by permission of Henry Holt and Company, LLC.

ISBN:978-0-615-24888-2

ONE ON A SIDE

A Reading and Lecture
by Seamus Heaney,
Recipient of the Nobel Prize in Literature

Oh, just another kind of outdoor game,

One on a side. It comes to little more:

There where it is we do not need the wall:

He is all pine and I am apple orchard.

—Robert Frost, from "Mending Wall"

It's great to be introduced by Jane Brox, and it's an honor to be your guest at the Frost Foundation. Jane is from north of Boston, and when I first encountered her poetry—not just her poetry in verse but the poetry that's in her prose as well—I was delighted by her at homeness in a familial landscape, her sense of ancestry, and the general emotional reliability this confers on her writing. And this kind of reliability, or authenticity, is something we recognize in Frost too. Yet in Frost there's roguery as well as authenticity: call it, if you like, authentic roguery—he himself called it "mischief." It comes, at any rate, from his inability to settle too trustingly or sedately into life in the world, his combination of wanting to be emotionally in place but also needing to be intellectually on the move.

This annual tribute to Frost, I should say, is admirable and exemplary, a community event which is equally an act of *pietas*, of devotedness. By coming together like this the community signifies that it values not just Frost but the activity Frost stood for. The activity of art, that is, of song and all that song entails. And those songs in the opening performance by the Lawrence High School Singers surely did add an extra sweetness to the program.

So: by coming and assembling you are celebrating not only Frost but yourselves. And that is one of the functions of art, especially the art of song and of poetry: it invites us to be at one together and to exult in being ourselves.
Frost got an honorary degree from Trinity College, Dublin, and when he was in Ireland he met the man who was at that stage the doyen of our poets, Austin Clarke,

also a very distinguished craftsman, somebody who would have appreciated the high sophistication that always lay behind Frost's beguiling simplicity. Anyhow, there was this famous exchange between them: Frost asks Clarke: "How do you write your poetry?"—always a difficult question—and Clarke replies, "I load myself with golden chains and try to escape." Meaning that he set himself a lot of technical challenges and tried to surmount them.

Frost himself was a master craftsman, something indeed of a wizard with words. The longer I read him the more I appreciate this wizardly side of him, his ability to weave a lyric spell, to conjure with the musical, mesmeric element in language. But I have to say that when I first came to his poetry, the side of Frost that absolutely riveted me was his resolute down-to-earthness—the Frost of things-as-they-are. The first poem of his that I remember encountering was the one called " 'Out, Out—'."
"Out, out, brief candle," says Macbeth,

"Life's but a walking shadow; a poor player,

That struts and frets his hour upon the stage,

And then is heard no more: it is a tale

Told by an idiot, full of sound and fury,

Signifying nothing."

(Shakespeare, *Macbeth*, Act 5, scene 5)

What happens in Frost's poem raises the question implicit in Macbeth's speech: what does it signify, our life here? This is also the question in Frost's mind when he tells of an accident in a New England farmyard. Suddenly, shockingly, a child loses his hand in a buzz-saw. That's it, a family loss, fierce and bewildering—but the family is left with no choice but to get on with their daily tasks.

I begin with this poem because I think it is completely available to the person who is utterly shy of poetry—and there still are a few of them around:

ONE ON A SIDE

'*Out, Out—*'

The buzz saw snarled and rattled in the yard
And made dust and dropped stove-length sticks of wood,
Sweet-scented stuff when the breeze drew across it.
And from there those that lifted eyes could count
Five mountain ranges one behind the other
Under the sunset far into Vermont.
And the saw snarled and rattled, snarled and rattled,
As it ran light, or had to bear a load.
And nothing happened: day was all but done.
Call it a day, I wish they might have said
To please the boy by giving him the half hour
That a boy counts so much when saved from work.
His sister stood beside them in her apron
To tell them 'Supper.' At the word, the saw,
As if to prove saws knew what supper meant,
Leaped out at the boy's hand, or seemed to leap—

He must have given the hand. However it was,
Neither refused the meeting. But the hand!
The boy's first outcry was a rueful laugh,
As he swung toward them holding up the hand
Half in appeal, but half as if to keep
The life from spilling. Then the boy saw all—
Since he was old enough to know, big boy
Doing a man's work, though a child at heart—
He saw all spoiled. 'Don't let him cut my hand off—
The doctor, when he comes. Don't let him, sister!'
So. But the hand was gone already.
The doctor put him in the dark of ether.
He lay and puffed his lips out with his breath.
And then—the watcher at his pulse took fright.
No one believed. They listened at his heart.
Little—less—nothing!—and that ended it.
No more to build on there. And they, since they
Were not the one dead, turned to their affairs.

(Frost, Robert. 'Out, Out—', *Mountain Interval,* 1916)

ONE ON A SIDE

The first time I heard that read it went home unforgettably, like the accident itself, into consciousness. But I also remember that there was a class discussion and the teacher proposed, maybe even believed, there was something callous about the end of the poem because, after this dreadful thing happened, the people, "since they/Were not the one dead, turned to their affairs." Thus the question was raised: was this continuation of things, this return to what had to be done, was this a failure? Some people said yes, definitely, but I remember making bold to say no, because I knew from my own experience of such accidents that all you can do the morning after the funeral is what you have always done, keep going and get on with it. Regretfully perhaps, perhaps stoically, but with a broken rather than a hardened heart. So for me that first poem had the shock of reality in it, and I will never forget it.

And there were other poems that attracted me in a similar way, because of their content. "Mowing," for instance, the early sonnet. I myself had learnt to mow and took pride in my ability to sharpen and handle a scythe. Come to think of it, there was a special kind of scythe shaft they often used in County Derry—and Frost of course was a Derry boy too—another connection there—a scythe that had a shaft with a curve in it. This curved handle was for some reason called a "Yankee sned" and it gave you a longer, lower sweep and cut. Anyway, I loved to mow, and loved to hear and watch other people mow, even when I had to fall in behind and lift and bind oats or grass-seed at the heels of the mower—the "swale," as Frost called it. So his poem meant a lot to me just because it described the particular sound of the blade in grass. I was delighted because the poet turned out to be a secret sharer of something I thought was intimately mine. Yet the poem isn't just about the fact of mowing: it's equally about the melody of it. About absorption in the task. About becoming entranced. In the end it's a defense of the kind of poem "Mowing" turns out to be: one that doesn't take you away and lead you into faeryland but keeps you on the earth, keeps you, as William Wordsworth said, "in the presence of flesh and blood," in the presence of labour.

ONE ON A SIDE

You are definitely in this world, not in the Garden of Eden, but outside Eden, where you earn your living by the sweat of your brow.... Frost conjures up a lovely cadenced music in his lines, not in order to create some dreamland fantasy, some background music of escape, but to recreate where we are now, living with the fact of labour, following the usual human round. And that music of what happens is characteristic and valuable in all of his work, and so "Mowing":

Mowing

There was never a sound beside the wood but one,
And that was my long scythe whispering to the ground.
What was it it whispered? I knew not well myself;
Perhaps it was something about the heat of the sun,
Something, perhaps, about the lack of sound—
And that was why it whispered and did not speak.
It was no dream of the gift of idle hours,
Or easy gold at the hand of fay or elf:
Anything more than the truth would have seemed too weak
To the earnest love that laid the swale in rows,
Not without feeble-pointed spikes of flowers
(Pale orchises), and scared a bright green snake.
The fact is the sweetest dream that labor knows.
My long scythe whispered and left the hay to make.

(Frost, Robert. "Mowing," *A Boy's Will*, 1913)

I've been asked to read some poems of my own as well as poems by Frost. It makes me uneasy, but I'll do it all the same.

I was susceptible to 'Out, Out—', the poem about the accident in the farmyard, because in 1940's rural Ulster people still talked about accidents like that even if they happened ten, twenty, forty miles away. There was a grapevine that was both in dread of those things and entirely fascinated by them. The more gruesome the more compelling. People being caught in a threshing machine, for example; or falling into a stone-breaking machine in some quarry.

The accident that happened in my own family was less terrible, but still grievous. One of my young brothers was killed in a road accident. I believe, however, that 'Out, Out—' and other Frost poems like it prepared me for the poem I would write. I thought I therefore ought to read "Mid-Term Break," which was written ten years after the event. I'm sure my familiarity and love of poems in *North of Boston,* such as "Death of the Hired Man" and more especially that terrible, true poem "Home Burial," encouraged me just to set things down as plainly as possible.

Mid-Term Break

I sat all morning in the college sick bay
Counting bells knelling classes to a close.
At two o'clock our neighbours drove me home.

In the porch I met my father crying—
He had always taken funerals in his stride—
And Big Jim Evans saying it was a hard blow.

The baby cooed and laughed and rocked the pram
When I came in, and I was embarrassed
By old men standing up to shake my hand

And tell me they were 'sorry for my trouble'.
Whispers informed strangers I was the eldest,
Away at school, as my mother held my hand

In hers and coughed out angry tearless sighs.
At ten o'clock the ambulance arrived
With the corpse, stanched and bandaged by the nurses.

Next morning I went up into the room. Snowdrops
And candles soothed the bedside; I saw him
For the first time in six weeks. Paler now,

Wearing a poppy bruise on his left temple,
He lay in the four foot box as in his cot.
No gaudy scars, the bumper knocked him clear.

A four foot box, a foot for every year.

(Heaney, Seamus. "Mid-Term Break," *Death of a Naturalist*, 1966)

One On A Side

"The fact is the sweetest dream labor knows."

I too wrote poems early on about craftsmen and their crafts, descriptions of labour which were equally images of artwork. They were Frostian in that they were very much involved in the workaday, but they were also admiring of the element of wizardry in the work they described, the magic touch, as it were. This one is about a thatcher. When I was growing up, thatching was still being done with wheat straw. It reversed the process of aging—the old gray-haired thatch became renewed and ended up a golden blonde. Thatching, in other words, produced a hair-dye effect long before I knew there was such a thing as hair-dye. An image of the artist at work, not mowing but thatching:

Thatcher

Bespoke for weeks, he turned up some morning
Unexpectedly, his bicycle slung
With a light ladder and a bag of knives.
He eyed the old rigging, poked at the eaves.

Opened and handled sheaves of lashed wheat-straw.
Next, the bundled rods: hazel and willow
Were flicked for weight, twisted in case they'd snap.
It seemed he spent the morning warming up:

Then fixed the ladder, laid out well-honed blades
And snipped at straw and sharpened ends of rods
That, bent in two, made a white-pronged staple
For pinning down his world, handful by handful.

Couchant for days on sods above the rafters,

He shaved and flushed the butts, stitched all together

Into a sloped honeycomb, a stubble patch,

And left them gaping at his Midas touch.

(Heaney, Seamus. "Thatcher," *Door Into the Dark*, 1969)

Frost, as I said earlier, left us gaping at his Midas touch very often, and nowhere more beautifully than in a poem called "A Hillside Thaw," which I heartily commend. It's one where he lets the cat out of the bag and then, as it were, puts the cat back in. It's about the way the morning sun thaws out a snowy landscape that has frozen under the moon at night, and then about the moon freezing it all over again. But equally, of course, it's about the pleasure Frost takes in the wizardry of his own description of these transformations, which appear as fluent and effortless in his language as they are in reality in the landscape.

The poem I want to read next, however, is as worldly as it is wizardly, and it eventually revealed an extra, truly worldly strength when I re-read it later in life. This was during the Troubles in Northern Ireland—troubles which often forced Northern Irish readers and writers to put whatever they read under extra pressure. They would test work for its reality quotient, as it were. And in this case "Mending Wall" stood up admirably. It's the one about the two farmers who live apart being forced to come together. It allows for and explores different attitudes to division and to borders, to living together and/or apart. Its great virtue is that it's true to life. It sustains interrogation like a truthful witness. And here it happens that there are truthful witnesses on both sides of the case. So the poem invites all kinds of interpretation. You can come down on one side or the other, but you don't have to. Which means that it can be read as a political poem. It certainly made sense when there was a peace line—a minding wall, so to speak—in Belfast; and it would make sense but give no consolation under the different walls in and around Israel:

ONE ON A SIDE

Mending Wall

Something there is that doesn't love a wall,
That sends the frozen-ground-swell under it,
And spills the upper boulders in the sun;
And makes gaps even two can pass abreast.
The work of hunters is another thing:
I have come after them and made repair
Where they have left not one stone on a stone,
But they would have the rabbit out of hiding,
To please the yelping dogs. The gaps I mean,
No one has seen them made or heard them made,
But at spring mending-time we find them there.
I let my neighbor know beyond the hill;
And on a day we meet to walk the line
And set the wall between us once again.
We keep the wall between us as we go.
To each the boulders that have fallen to each.
And some are loaves and some so nearly balls

We have to use a spell to make them balance:

'Stay where you are until our backs are turned!'

We wear our fingers rough with handling them.

Oh, just another kind of outdoor game,

One on a side. It comes to little more:

There where it is we do not need the wall:

He is all pine and I am apple orchard.

My apple trees will never get across

And eat the cones under his pines, I tell him.

He only says, 'Good fences make good neighbors.'

Spring is the mischief in me, and I wonder

If I could put a notion in his head:

'*Why* do they make good neighbors? Isn't it

Where there are cows? But here there are no cows.

Before I built a wall I'd ask to know

What I was walling in or walling out,

And to whom I was like to give offense.

Something there is that doesn't love a wall,

One On A Side

That wants it down!' I could say 'Elves' to him,
But it's not elves exactly, and I'd rather
He said it for himself. I see him there
Bringing a stone grasped firmly by the top
In each hand, like an old-stone savage armed.
He moves in darkness as it seems to me,
Not of woods only and the shade of trees.
He will not go behind his father's saying,
And he likes having thought of it so well
He says again, 'Good fences make good neighbors.'

(Frost, Robert. "Mending Wall," *North of Boston*, 1914)

That poem, as it happens, relates to one I wrote called "The Other Side," again set between two farms that shared the one boundary, in this case a small overgrown stream. A "march," meaning a border, as in The Welsh Marches, between Wales and England.

"The Other Side" begins with a memory of myself as a youngster in the presence of a grand old patriarchal neighbour called Johnny Junkin. He did look like a patriarch: the black waistcoat, the gray hat, the white moustache. He was Presbyterian and his reading was the Bible, so he spoke a language full of Biblical names and instances—Jacob, Isaac, the Pharaoh, and so on. We, on the other hand—on the other side, indeed—were Catholics; and as is often the case with Irish Catholics, our talk was larded with exclamations in the holy name of the hero of The New Testament.

This poem is about the divisions that were always under the surface of Ulster life, but it's also about the negotiations they entailed. Not across a wall, but a little farm drain or stream. The phrase "the other side" was part of the Ulster vernacular for a long time. It belonged in our discourse well before the theoretical "Other" entered the language of the postgraduate seminar.

The Other Side

I
Thigh-deep in sedge and marigolds,
a neighbour laid his shadow
on the stream, vouching

'It's as poor as Lazarus, that ground,'
and brushed away
among the shaken leafage.

I lay where his lea sloped
to meet our fallow,
nested on moss and rushes,

my ear swallowing
his fabulous, biblical dismissal,
that tongue of chosen people.

ONE ON A SIDE

>
> When he would stand like that
> on the other side, white-haired,
> swinging his blackthorn
>
> at the marsh weeds,
> he prophesied above our scraggy acres,
> then turned away
>
> towards his promised furrows
> on the hill, a wake of pollen
> drifting to our bank, next season's tares.
>
> II
> For days we would rehearse
> each patriarchal dictum:
> Lazarus, the Pharaoh, Solomon
>
> and David and Goliath rolled
> magnificently, like loads of hay
> too big for our small lanes,

or faltered on a rut—
'Your side of the house, I believe,
hardly rule by the Book at all.'

His brain was a whitewashed kitchen
hung with texts, swept tidy
as the body o' the kirk.

III

Then sometimes when the rosary was dragging
mournfully on in the kitchen
we would hear his step round the gable

though not until after the litany
would the knock come to the door
and the casual whistle strike up

on the doorstep. 'A right-looking night,'
he might say, 'I was dandering by
and says I, I might as well call.'

One On A Side

But now I stand behind him
in the dark yard, in the moan of prayers.
He puts a hand in a pocket

or taps a little tune with the blackthorn
shyly, as if he were party to
lovemaking or a stranger's weeping.

Should I slip away, I wonder,
or go up and touch his shoulder
and talk about the weather

or the price of grass-seed?

(Heaney, Seamus. "The Other Side," *Wintering Out*, 1972)

One of the most beautiful poems in the language is "After Apple Picking." It has grown so familiar that we forget what an extraordinary achievement it is. Mysterious and plain: completely at one with the fact of apple-picking, the ladder rung hurting the instep-arch, the rumble of the emptying barrels, then the mesmeric sway, the dreaminess, the sheet of ice held so that the world turns almost hallucinatory. The child in you holds up the ice again and you remember that slight transformation, the first time perhaps you saw the world differently.

As usual, Frost remains true to things as they are on this earth, but he's true also to what he called "the sound of sense," true to the ear as well as to the earth—for there is always a deeply attentive EAR in Frost's EARth.

"After Apple Picking" invites comparison with another poem of harvest, John Keats's "When I have fears that I may cease to be," full as it is of grain and garnering, full of the same rich anticipation and creative brio, another little allegory of the artist's life. Also, I've often thought that a suitable epigraph for "After Apple Picking" might be one of my favourite quotations from Czeslaw Milosz: "What articulates itself, strengthens itself. What is not articulated tends to non-being."

I love too the sound of the old rogue's voice as he reads it. I never had the good fortune to hear Frost in person, but in the 1960s I often listened to a Caedmon LP recording which included this poem and "Birches." I loved the hard clear articulation, the wonderful switch-back come and go of his pacing.

After Apple Picking

My long two-pointed ladder's sticking through a tree
Toward heaven still,
And there's a barrel that I didn't fill
Beside it, and there may be two or three
Apples I didn't pick upon some bough.
But I am done with apple-picking now.
Essence of winter sleep is on the night,
The scent of apples: I am drowsing off.
I cannot rub the strangeness from my sight
I got from looking through a pane of glass
I skimmed this morning from the drinking trough
And held against the world of hoary grass.
It melted, and I let it fall and break.
But I was well
Upon my way to sleep before it fell,
And I could tell

One On A Side

What form my dreaming was about to take.

Magnified apples appear and disappear,

Stem end and blossom end,

And every fleck of russet showing clear.

My instep arch not only keeps the ache,

It keeps the pressure of a ladder-round.

I feel the ladder sway as the boughs bend.

And I keep hearing from the cellar bin

The rumbling sound

Of load on load of apples coming in.

For I have had too much

Of apple-picking: I am overtired

Of the great harvest I myself desired.

There were ten thousand thousand fruit to touch,

Cherish in hand, lift down, and not let fall.

For all

That struck the earth,

No matter if not bruised or spiked with stubble,

Went surely to the cider-apple heap

As of no worth.
One can see what will trouble
This sleep of mine, whatever sleep it is.

Were he not gone,

The woodchuck could say whether it's like his

Long sleep, as I describe its coming on,

Or just some human sleep.

(Frost, Robert. "After Apple-Picking," *North of Boston*, 1914)

ONE ON A SIDE

Stories like that, half in the world of dream but still completely credible as accounts of the world of the actual—those are the kinds of poem I particularly like. And I'd hope that some of the ones I've written have a similar quality. So I'm going to read three more of my own.

The following is Part III of a triptych called "Seeing Things." It's a memory of seeing my father not through a pane of ice but through a window pane. He came into the yard looking strange just as I was looking out. He had almost drowned that day while working with a horse and horse-sprayer in our riverbank field. Earlier on I had wanted to go with him but was not allowed. What I always remember is the strangeness of seeing him come back somehow changed. Apart from anything else, he had lost his hat—it had been washed away in the river—so it was like seeing Hermes bareheaded. Part III of "Seeing Things":

ONE ON A SIDE

from *Seeing Things*

Once upon a time my undrowned father
Walked into our yard. He had gone to spray
Potatoes in a field on the riverbank
And wouldn't bring me with him. The horse-sprayer
Was too big and new-fangled, bluestone might
Burn me in the eyes, the horse was fresh, I
Might scare the horse, and so on. I threw stones
At a bird on the shed roof, as much for
The clatter of the stones as anything,
But when he came back, I was inside the house
And saw him out the window, scatter-eyed
And daunted, strange without his hat,
His step unguided, his ghosthood immanent.
When he was turning on the riverbank,
The horse had rusted and reared up and pitched
Cart and sprayer and everything off balance

So the whole rig went over into a deep

Whirlpool, hoofs, chains, shafts, cartwheels, barrel

And tackle, all tumbling off the world,

And the hat already merrily swept along

The quieter reaches. That afternoon

I saw him face to face, he came to me

With his damp footprints out of the river,

And there was nothing between us there

That might not still be happily ever after.

(Heaney, Seamus. Part III of "Seeing Things," *Seeing Thing*s, 1991)

The next is another between-two-worlds poem, although in this case there's no ladder swaying on an apple bough, no birch bough letting a boy down and then bringing him up. Something far more wonderful occurs, although the tone of the storytelling is entirely matter of fact. And the tone is something I picked up from the original source in the early medieval annals of the monastery of Clonmacnoise in Ireland. What I liked about the entry in the annals was the fact that the writing was plain and unfazed but the tale it told was astonishing:

from *Lightenings*

The annals say: when the monks of Clonmacnoise
Were all at prayers inside the oratory
A ship appeared above them in the air.

The anchor dragged along behind so deep
It hooked itself into the altar rails
And then, as the big hull rocked to a standstill,

A crewman shinned and grappled down the rope
And struggled to release it. But in vain.
'This man can't bear our life here and will drown,'

The abbot said, 'unless we help him.' So
They did, the freed ship sailed, and the man climbed back
Out of the marvellous as he had known it.

(Heaney, Seamus. Part VIII of "Lightenings," *Seeing Things*, 1991)

This next poem speaks for itself. It is a meditation on a story. An old Irish tale about Saint Kevin and the blackbird. Those old Irish saints, I should tell you, prayed with their arms held out wide, so that their bodies resembled the form of a cross:

St Kevin and the Blackbird

And then there was St Kevin and the blackbird.
The saint is kneeling, arms stretched out, inside
His cell, but the cell is narrow, so

One turned-up palm is out the window, stiff
As a crossbeam, when a blackbird lands
And lays in it and settles down to nest.

Kevin feels the warm eggs, the small breast, the tucked
Neat head and claws and, finding himself linked
Into the network of eternal life,

Is moved to pity: now he must hold his hand
Like a branch out in the sun and rain for weeks
Until the young are hatched and fledged and flown.

★∧★

ONE ON A SIDE

> And since the whole thing's imagined anyhow,
>
> Imagine being Kevin. Which is he?
>
> Self-forgetful or in agony all the time
>
> From the neck on out down through his hurting forearms?
>
> Are his fingers sleeping? Does he still feel his knees?
>
> Or has the shut-eyed blank of underearth
>
> Crept up through him? Is there distance in his head?
>
> Alone and mirrored clear in love's deep river,
>
> 'To labour and not to seek reward,' he prays,
>
> A prayer his body makes entirely
>
> For he has forgotten self, forgotten bird
>
> And on the riverbank forgotten the river's name.
>
> (Heaney, Seamus. "St Kevin and the Blackbird,"
>
> *The Spirit Level*, 1996)

Finally, two Frost poems. "To Earthward," like the poem about Saint Kevin, is about testing one's capacity for endurance, one's adequacy when faced with hard reality. It's a love poem about taking the full strain and pain that love entails. The poet is saying that he has got to a point where he almost needs to be hurt if an experience, even the experience of love, is to be credible. In order for things to show up true, they have to press down hard on him. And he has to press down hard on them. This is one of Frost's very best:

To Earthward

Love at the lips was touch
As sweet as I could bear;
And once that seemed too much;
I lived on air

That crossed me from sweet things,
The flow of—was it musk
From hidden grapevine springs
Downhill at dusk?

I had the swirl and ache
From sprays of honeysuckle
That when they're gathered shake
Dew on the knuckle.

I craved strong sweets, but those
Seemed strong when I was young;
The petal of the rose
It was that stung.

Now no joy but lacks salt
That is not dashed with pain
And weariness and fault;
I crave the stain

Of tears, the aftermark
Of almost too much love,
The sweet of bitter bark
And burning clove.

When stiff and sore and scarred
I take away my hand
From leaning on it hard
In grass and sand,

The hurt is not enough:
I long for weight and strength
To feel the earth as rough
To all my length.

(Frost, Robert. "To Earthward," *New Hampshire*, 1923)

ONE ON A SIDE

Still, for all his affinity with the roughness of life, Frost remains, like Saint Kevin with the blackbird, linked into life's most tender circuits. It's all implicit in that lovely feminine rhyme of "honeysuckle" and "knuckle." Which is why I want to end with a tender-hearted little poem called "The Runaway." It too contains both sides of his sensibility, the part that is fully aware of the hard lot life can offer us all, human and animal alike, and the part that is susceptible to the pathos of all that is exposed and vulnerable:

The Runaway

Once when the snow of the year was beginning to fall,
We stopped by a mountain pasture to say, 'Whose colt?'
A little Morgan had one forefoot on the wall,
The other curled at his breast. He dipped his head
And snorted to us. And then we saw him bolt.
We heard the miniature thunder where he fled,
And we saw him, or thought we saw him, dim and gray,
Like a shadow across instead of behind the flakes.
'I think the little fellow's afraid of the snow.
He isn't winter broken. It isn't play
With the little fellow at all. He's running away.
I doubt if even his mother could tell him, "Sakes,
It's only weather." He'd think she didn't know!
Where is his mother? He can't be out alone.'
And now he comes again with a clatter of stone,
And mounts the wall again with whited eyes
And all his tail that isn't hair up straight.

He shudders his coat as if to throw off flies.

'Whoever it is that leaves him out so late,

When other creatures have gone to stall and bin,

Ought to be told to come and take him in.'

(Frost, Robert. "The Runaway," *New Hampshire*, 1923)

Seamus Heaney kindly agreed that all proceeds from this newly edited version of the original lecture will be donated to the Robert Frost Foundation for the support of community poetry activities in Lawrence, Massachusetts.

We gratefully acknowledge Jonathan Galassi at Farrar, Straus, and Giroux and Mimi Ross at Henry Holt and Company for permission to include the Heaney and Frost poems quoted by Seamus Heaney. For photographs, special thanks to Louise Sandberg at the Lawrence Public Library, Laura Burnham, chair of the Frost Farm at Derry and members of the Frost and Heaney families.

Photo captions:

Dust jacket, p. 2, p. 38, and p. 54 Seamus Heaney at Lawrence High School, Massachusetts, on October 26, 2002. 2002 © Neil Hamburg.

P. 12 Robert Frost mowing in Derry, NH. Courtesy of the Trustees of the Frost Farm at Derry, NH.

P. 18 Seamus Heaney and his son Michael at The Wood, Bellaghy, c. 1973 © Jim Bennett.

P. 27 Robert Frost in New Hampshire (Lotti Jacobi) Courtesy of the Trustees of the Frost Farm at Derry, NH.

P. 50 Haverhill Street in Lawrence, Masschsetts Collection of Lawrence Public Libary.

ONE ON A SIDE

www.ingramcontent.com/pod-product-compliance
Lightning Source LLC
Chambersburg PA
CBHW031358160426

42813CB00090B/3206/J